THE ADVENTURE
OF JUDAISM

THE ADVENTURE OF JUDAISM

THREE
CONFIRMATION SERVICES

By

RABBI ABRAHAM J. FELDMAN

BEHRMAN'S JEWISH BOOK HOUSE

Publishers   1 9 3 7   *New York*

Preface

I have been asked to publish some of the confirmation services which, in the course of my ministry, I had prepared. These, given herewith, are selected at random from the collection.

It should be said that these services are based, structurally, on the very unusual Confirmation Service which was devised by the late Rabbi Joseph Krauskopf of Philadelphia, with whom the present writer was associated for a number of years in the ministry of the Reform Congregation Keneseth Israel, in that city.

A few explanations of items in the service may be helpful.

The Confirmands as they enter the Temple carry with them a Bible, a Prayer Book, Six White Rosebuds and a symbol of human service which is in the form of a small "Mogen Dovid" pin of gold and black enamel with the word "Service" in gold in the center of the figure. The six corners of the star have the initials of the congregation (Beth Israel Confirmation Class), and the year of confirmation, in this wise:

These serve, also, as class-pins, and are greatly cherished by the young people. In the joy of officiating at the marriages of these Confirmands, I have had the great satisfaction of seeing, invariably, this beautiful and significant symbol fastened onto the bridal gown or the bridegroom's lapel or vest.

The charge of the Rabbi to the Confirmation Class leads up to the significance of these symbols and at the conclusion of the charge, they are returned to the members of the class.

When the Confirmands approach the altar for their blessing, each carries one of the Six White Rosebuds which is deposited in the Ark. These are later pressed and mounted with the name of each child thereon and are kept in a separate container in the Ark, perpetually.

At no time are the addresses given by the children repeated by other children in subsequent years. Each year's service is unique and stands by itself. The procedure usually is as follows: The Rabbi determines the general themes and the topics on which the children are to speak, depending upon the number of children in the Confirmation Class. The children then either select or are assigned their respective parts. Upon receiving their parts, a conference is arranged between each child and the Rabbi to discuss the possibilities of the respective themes. The children then attempt to write their own essays. These they return to the Rabbi who corrects or revises or rewrites, as the need may be. There are times when the children submit really thoughtful essays and only minor corrections are necessary. At other times, it is necessary for the Rabbi to discard what the children submit and to write out what the theme calls for. Always it is necessary to link the addresses into a continuity of thought.

The services as here published, are given in full, exactly as they were on the respective confirmation days, so that the complete value and unity of each may be seen.

If these are found acceptable, perhaps another and larger group of services may be published at a later time.

A. J. F.

Hartford, Conn.
Purim, 5697—February 25, 1937

Contents

THIRD SERVICE

THE ADVENTURE
OF JUDAISM

Confirmation Service

I

ORGAN PRELUDE

VIOLIN SOLO

SHABUOTH SERVICE
(Union Prayer Book, pages 206-220, 229, 238)

PROCESSIONAL (Organ)—Coronation March from
"Le Prophete" ....*Meyerbeer*

[*Escorted by Confirmands of other years and Officers of the Congregation, the Confirmands enter the Temple, each bearing a Bible, a Prayer Book, Six White Rosebuds, and an Emblem of Human Service. The Congregation is requested not to rise during the Processional.*]

CHOIR:

How blessed are, how blessed are who come in the name of the
    Lord our God!
Oh, bless'd be ye, oh, bless'd be ye, in the house of the Lord our
    God!
How blessed are, who come in the name of the Lord our God!
Oh, bless'd be ye, in the house of the Lord our God.

OPENING PRAYER

CREATOR OF ALL:

We, the Confirmands, approach this altar reverently and with joyous awe. This is the day Thou hast made. We thank Thee for it, O God. Well do we realize how great is the debt

1

we owe Thee. All that we have—art not Thou the giver of all our blessings, the blessings of devoted parents, of loving relatives, of loyal friends; the blessings of homes and comforts, of food and shelter and security. We are truly grateful for these. But even more grateful are we on this day for those blessings which are not external, but are within us. For Thy revelation of Thyself unto our fathers and unto us; for Thy law of righteousness which Thou didst implant in our hearts; for our sense of right and the desire to know the right. We thank Thee for the teachings of prophets and sages inspired by Thee, and transmitted to us. We thank Thee for Thy choice of Israel to be Thy servant, Thy priest and prophet. We thank Thee for the inspiring records of faithfulness which our people's history contains, for our people's loyalty and sacrificial devotion.

And we pray Thee, our Father, as we ascend this altar, to give us the strength and the courage, the wisdom and power to be as faithful as were our fathers, as loyal as they were, as true.

Help us, O God, to rise worthily to the challenge of this day and hour, and vowing undying faithfulness as we do, that we remain steadfast to our pledge. May we demonstrate our conviction of Thy truths in our everyday actions, so that we may carry the inspiration of this sacred ceremony of Confirmation into our lives, and through our deeds give happiness to our parents, joy to our Rabbi, strength to our Congregation, and hope to our people and mankind. Amen.

[*Confirmands deposit within shrine: Bible, Prayer Book, Emblem of Human Service and Six White Rosebuds.*]

OUR CONFIRMATION

If life be a struggle and only the fittest survive, then is confirmation but the procedure of sending reinforcements, trained, enthusiastic, eager souls, into the battle lines of Jewish life.

We, of this year's class, in this congregation and in the thousands of other congregations throughout the land, are new recruits joyously entering the lines, and our confirmation service is the rite of initiation and induction during which we pledge our allegiance to God, to Judaism and to Jewish life.

We pledge ourselves only after a long period of preparation. For nine years have we been trained and instructed in the history of our people, its traditions and hopes, and during the past year, under our Rabbi's guidance, in the ethics and doctrines of Judaism. We come voluntarily to affirm publicly the truth revealed to us. We confirm today the teachings of the past. We pledge ourselves to strengthen Judaism by our faith and to give vitality to Jewish life by our lives.

This is not a graduation, unless it be a commencement of our responsibility for Jewish living. This is the ancient Bar Mitzvah ceremony expanded to include all, youths and maidens of Israel.

We are confirmed in our convictions and we confirm because of our convictions. We are tremendously in earnest, and we ask for your prayers in our behalf, and for your sustaining example in loyalty—as we go forth into life.

OUR FAITH

In One God

The belief in one God originated with the ancient Hebrews. This doctrine of monotheism was totally different from the beliefs concerning gods held by other religions of antiquity. The other ancient peoples worshipped gods of the sun, the moon, the wind, and the rain. To their religiously crude minds, these phenomena were mysterious and unfathomable and they were incapable of reasoning beyond their sense experiences. And so they accepted them as sources of life rather than consequences, and proclaimed each in turn as the great Source. It was the ancient Hebrews who first recognized that these elements or planets could not be ultimate sources and proceeded to the discovery of God—as the invisible yet real, the spiritual not physical Being back of all life. They proceeded to worship the Creator—*not* the created. They believed that *one* God reigns supreme. They reasoned that there cannot be two or more gods, for if there were, no perfect harmony or unity would exist either in the heavens or on the earth.

How do we know there *is* a God? We know there is a God because we *feel* Him, and see evidences of His revelation and of His will everywhere. He revealed Himself to our fathers of old, and He continues to reveal Himself to our hearts and minds today. How can we behold all the beauties of nature and not see and praise Him who brought it all about? Is there not a greater being who created and controls all these powers? These could not merely have "happened."

But God is not just a one-time Creator, who started all, and did nothing since. He is a perpetual God, perpetually creating, living and working with us, and within us, and through us. He is not an indifferent, absentee God. He is with everyone, sustaining us and helping us, an ever-present ruler, guiding and instructing us always.

We, the younger generation, should uphold this glorious belief in the Almighty; we should love Him and proclaim His power. Ours is the mission to vitalize the faith of our fathers and make God an ideal ever more real to us and to others. And as we honestly endeavor to cast aside those idols which many, today, worship instead of the God of all life, the idols of greed and power and pleasure, our lives will become, must become, each a noble effort and a great spiritual adventure, a pride to all our dear ones, a blessing to all men, and above all a delight to our Maker, the One and Only God.

In One Humanity

Believing as we do, in the unity of God, and in God as the creator of all, it follows,—does it not?—that we are all brethren and kin of the same family, children of the same great Father. Therefore, we should feel as children of one little circle do. Hatred and malice, treachery and double dealing, enmity and discord should have no place among men. To permit these, to yield to them, to encourage them, is to deny God's fatherhood and His moral precepts. "Have we not all one father?" asked one of our prophets; "Hath not one God created us? Why then do we deal treacherously one man with his brother, and profane the covenant of our fathers?" God has no darlings amongst men. He loves all men alike. He shows no special favors. And He expects men to serve His great purpose of working and serving and living together as brothers. Races may differ—but only as complexions may vary in the same household, as temperaments may vary amongst brothers and sisters of the same family. People dwell in different countries and mistrust each other and dislike each other—yet should there be no greater difference between them than there is between married brothers and sisters of the same family each of whom has his or her own household, and are yet united in their common origin, their common source.

If, then, God is one, and He is the Father of all men, Humanity must be one, and all men brethren, children of the one Father of all.

This doctrine the Jew has always taught. This doctrine we accept as an article of our faith today. And we go forth in the hope that in the not-too-distant future, the Psalmist's declaration will become the joyous chant of mankind united:

"Behold, how good and how pleasant it is, for brethren to dwell together in unity."

In Peace Universal

Out of the belief in One God and in One Humanity, the belief in Universal Peace is born.

It was the great prophets of Israel who first spoke of universal peace, and they conceived of it as that peace which would unite all men and pervade the whole universe. Thus, Isaiah pictured the Messianic time as the period in which all men will walk in the path of God; when *He* will judge between the nations and peoples, and war will be known no longer.

Peace is glorified, by the Rabbis, as one of the greatest blessings that man may attain. It is one of the pillars of the world; without it the social order could not exist.

We are not only to be peaceful ourselves, but to help others to be peaceful.

This duty has wide implications. Peace ought to be not only a personal, but a national and international ideal. War is so terrible a calamity, so dark a blot upon our civilization, that the greatest efforts should be made to avert it. There are worse things, it is true, than war; but the worst of them all is the belief that war is indispensable, that there are international differences which cannot be adjusted without it, that its entire abolition is impossible. Such a belief is fatal to the ultimate establishment of universal peace.

The Jew who is true to himself will labor with especial energy in the cause of peace. His religion, his history, his mission all pledge him to a policy of peace, as a citizen as well as an individual. The Jew's task is to sow not strife, but brotherly love, among men; he has been called in order to bring, not a sword, but peace. And the true follower of the prophets is he only who sees with them, Peace Universal as the keystone of the gateway which leads into that Golden Age and blessed state when and where nation will not lift up sword against nation, nor learn war any more.

HYMN

[The Congregation is requested to rise and join in the singing of this and subsequent hymns.]

Father of Life and Light and Pow'r,
To Thee we consecrate this hour!
With earnest hope, with purpose pure,
O make this happy promise sure.

Help us to lay foundations strong
Of love for right, of grief for wrong;
And brotherhood with every race
That seeks or needs the Father's grace.

Help us to grow in pure desires,
Kindle our souls with heavenly fires,
That higher levels may be won
And step by step Thy will be done.

Build in us all Thy spirit's shrine,
Then shall we beam with light divine,
"And work with heart and soul and might
For Truth and Freedom, God and Right."

THE TORAH SERVICE
(Union Prayer Book, page 248)

BENEDICTION BEFORE READING FROM SCROLL

SCRIPTURE READING—TEN COMMANDMENTS (in Hebrew)

TRANSLATION OF TEN COMMANDMENTS

BENEDICTION AFTER READING FROM SCROLL

THE HAPHTARAH (Isaiah 42:1-12)

RETURNING OF THE SCROLL TO THE SHRINE
(Union Prayer Book, page 270)

OUR ETHICS

THE SANCTITY OF ALL LIFE

Judaism teaches the sanctity of all life. The commandment "Thou shalt not murder" forbids not only the conscious taking of life—whether slaying others or taking one's own life, but bids us avoid doing anything that might endanger life or even health. Judaism considers life God's greatest gift, a gift which man cannot create and therefore must neither destroy nor abuse nor endanger. Every life—so have we been taught—has value. Every life has significance for others, for society. Every life has a function to fulfill and that function means strength and service to other men. Because of such value and significance, because of its divine origin, and because of its great purpose—life is sacred. This imposes upon us obligations. To preserve our health and the health of others is one of these obligations. To do everything in our power to safeguard life and take every possible precaution against danger to it, to help in the stamping out of disease, to do nothing that would keep people from the proper enjoyment of it or making proper use of it, to refrain from silly worry and fretting, are other obligations. And to lead life in such a way as not to have anything impure soil it, anything indecent pollute it, anything dishonorable profane it, to keep anything and everything unworthy from disfiguring it—this is to recognize life's holiness. And to *prove* that holiness it is our duty not only to avoid evil but to render such useful service as to make it a blessing to all other lives.

RESPECT FOR THE EXPERIENCE OF THE RACE

Oliver Wendell Holmes once said, "We are like omnibuses driven by our ancestors," and he spoke truly. For it has been pointed out to us in the course of our studies that we are not only born with certain predispositions acquired through our ancestry, but also, that we are each born into a society composed of at least two others—our parents. This society has had certain experiences in living which are placed to our use, and are intended to spare us some of the bitterness and pain which are the price paid for such experiences. These experiences are expressed in the form of laws of conduct, and are communicated to us at first by our parents and others in the family. Then others are taught us by teachers to whom our parents have given of their authority. Then through the laws of the city, state and nation which also are formulated through the sanction and approval of all parents who give of their authority to their representatives acting for them.

It follows, therefore, that it behooves us to avail ourselves of this mass of past experience. We need not experiment with poison to discover its effects upon us. We need not court indecency to learn of its certain dangers. We need not—as Jews—flirt with assimilation to find out that we can thus endanger our very existence. "Honor thy father and thy mother that thy days may be long, and that it may go well with thee." Honor those whom father and mother have entrusted with thy well-being and education. Honor those whom thy parents and others' parents have set up in authority. These teachings of Judaism and their implications we were taught to believe—and we do believe—are safeguards of life, and as we live by them we can in a very large measure assure our happiness and the happiness of our neighbors.

THE OBLIGATION TO LABOR

Much stress has been laid upon the need of rest on one day out of each week. And it is right that this should be stressed. Man is not a soul-less machine; he needs time and opportunity for the re-creation of energies burned up. But even as important as is a weekly day of rest, so is it important to remember that without labor preceding it rest has no particular meaning.

The fourth commandment bids us not only to rest on the seventh day, but also "Six days *shalt* thou labor and do all thy work." Labor is as much a sacred task as the Sabbath is a needed day. Judaism teaches us that man must not be a parasite. He must create, he must produce, he must contribute to the lives of others. He must work and toil. Whether he work in the shop or in the mine, in the factory or behind the counter, in the office or in the school, in the hospital or in the court of justice, in the pulpit or in the newspaper office, in the studio or in the laboratory, in the nursery, in the kitchen, in the home —wherever one serves and whatever one does, insofar as one contributes to life's beauty or happiness or dignity or other needs, one labors and produces. It is a duty one fulfills. And only he knows the value of rest and its blessing who labors faithfully and diligently.

HONESTY

Honesty—which Judaism teaches as one of its cardinal ethical doctrines—is not alone a matter of not taking from others, without their knowledge, the property which is theirs. It means much more. For the employer, it means giving to the employee a fair and just share of the fruit of his labors. For the employee, it means giving full and faithful service to his employer. For all people, it means faithful devotion to duty, faithful adherence to obligations assumed. It means being what one would like to appear to be. It means the conscious avoidance of misrepresentation of any kind. It means giving recognition to those who are entitled to it, and not claiming as one's own what rightfully belongs to another.

Honesty thus is more than a social amenity. It is more than a good policy. It is not a matter of fear of punishment or of detection. It is a fundamental fact on which civilization rests, and without which faith neither in God nor men, neither honor nor security nor permanence, is possible.

REGARD FOR THE REPUTATION OF OTHERS

"Thou shalt not bear false witness against thy neighbor." This is a basic principle of human conduct. It recognizes the fact that the most precious possession any human being has— next to life itself—is one's reputation. Wealth may be had and lost and regained; health may sometimes be lost and regained; learning may or may not be of consequence. But one's good name lost, one's reputation besmirched, one's character bespattered—and all the wealth one may possess, all the learning one may acquire, all the health one might enjoy, do not overbalance the loss. To rob one of his good name is to disarm one in the midst of life's struggle and to leave him mortally wounded on the battlefield. It is a cowardly act at best; it is a criminal act when done unjustly and without cause.

To lend a ready ear to rumor unfounded; to respect the rumor; to be a party to gossip by receiving it, or communicating it; to slander a person or to libel an individual or a whole people —is to fail in this regard for the reputation of others. For death and life are in the power of the tongue and pen. Yes, more. A knowing shrug of the shoulders, a malicious raising of an eyebrow, the failure to deny what one knows to be an untruth or to believe what one does not know to be the truth—these have ruined more reputations and blasted more lives, have brought more unhappiness and caused more tears, have broken more hearts and homes than all the wars of history. For the false word spoken, the wrong impression given or approved, not all the denials or corrections can remove. To the one who sees or hears the denial a dozen have heard or seen the original statement.

The tale-bearer and slanderer are amongst the destructive elements of our population. For they fly in the face of that race experience which found expression in the ancient maxim of Jewry: "A good name is more to be desired than great riches."

HYMN

Lord, before Thy sacred Altar
    At the Temple's holy shrine,
Come Thy children with devotion
    To beseech Thy grace divine.
Here we pledge our consecration
    To the Law Thou didst reveal.
O may nations all revere it
    As life's holiest ideal.

O confirm our faith's devotion
    To Thy sacred Law of truth;
To the vow our fathers rendered
    In our people's early youth.
So we vow, in faith enduring,
    To be steadfast to the trust,
Which at Sinai they accepted,
    Which accept we will and must.

And while men in great contention
    Still withhold to sing Thy praise,
May Thine ancient faithful people,
    Lead the nations in Thy ways.
As our fathers greatly suffering,
    Gave up all to do Thy will,
So may we as loyal children,
    Loyal be and faithful still.

OUR LITERATURE

OUR BIBLE

The source of Jewish faith, of Jewish ethics, of Jewish idealism, the source which transmits these to us and preserves these for us, is found in the literature of the Jew. The records of soul-groping after God, the records of ideal standards of conduct, the records of the Jew's hope concerning the future of civilization—are found in our literature. And of all the vast mass of Jewish literature, the Bible is the oldest, the best known and the most inspiring.

Whatever people may think of the origin of the Bible, whether literally inspired or man-created, the fact remains that in it we find an account of our people rising spiritually from primitive notions of God and morality to the highest ideals as yet conceived by man. There we behold the rise of Israel to the belief in God as the God of the universe rather than that of a small territory, the God of mankind rather than the God of only one small people. It is there that we find recorded in simple narrative and inspired words of sage and saint—the truths of spiritual life that guide, thrill and uplift. It is there that we find the passionate cry against injustice as voiced by prophets, and the sweet consolation and resignation of the psalmists; the beautiful allegories of Ruth and Jonah as well as the gentle cynicism of Koheleth; the sins of the great denounced alike with the weakness of the small, the doubts of saints and the faith of the simple; the love of man and the love of God.

It is the book of civilized man. It helped to civilize him and make him strong. It is the book of human aspirations poured forth through the heart and soul of the Jew. It is the book of the Jew.

OUR TALMUD

The Jew never lived in the past alone. He has a supreme regard for the past, but he has a wholesome respect for the present as well. And when the past does not entirely meet the needs of the present, the Jew reverently takes the inspiring message of the past and modifies it to the needs of the present.

Thus when the Bible canon was closed, new needs arose which the old Bible could not exactly cover. The Rabbis, therefore, used the Bible, much as the Supreme Court of the United States uses our Federal Constitution—namely, they interpreted the Bible to meet the changing conditions. They established rules and regulations for daily living and conduct, they explained and modified, occasionally changed and abrogated the older law to suit the new concepts of the Jews.

The Talmud is the record of the discussions and decisions of the Rabbis extending over a period of over a thousand years. But it contains also the maxims and wise sayings and observations of life of those teachers, it reflects the moral point of view, the ideals, the hopes, the prayers, the customs, the traditions, the folk-lore, the legends, the history of the people of their day. It represents a later development of Jewish thought and for thousands of years our people have studied the Talmud, guided their lives by its teachings, found relaxation in its keen discussions, and in a very real sense, recognized it and used it as their second Bible.

OUR PHILOSOPHERS

The time came, at the end of the sixth century, when the Talmud was completed. And again, the living present made its demands. It was not satisfied with mere worship of the greatness of the past. And so the great Jewish philosophers of the Middle Ages came to meet the new conditions, to adjust Judaism to the newer point of view. And so Saadya came, and Bahyah, and, the greatest of them all, Moses Maimonides. Keen of mind, penetrating of intellect, learned and versed in the secular thought and sciences of their days, they related the teachings of the Bible and of the Rabbis to the thought of Arabic and Greek philosophers and harmonized them, pointing out that Jewish culture was not inconsistent with the best of secular world culture.

Their writings—which have come down to us—are monuments to their genius, to their depth of thought, to their progressive point of view, to their liberalism, to their learning. And our people, *nurtured* by them, have continued not apart from life, but in the very midst of world life, influencing and being influenced, constantly refreshed by the newer thought, but ever faithful to the fundamental, the profound lessons and ideals of the past; changing the outer shell, preserving the kernel, grasping the beauty of the new and holding *tenaciously* to the values of the old.

And, after all, is not this the method of true progress?

Our Poets

"The finest poetry was first experience," said Emerson, and this is peculiarly true of the great poets of our people. They sang of nature and of love, of joy and of sorrow, of triumph and defeat. But always, their poetry expressed not only their personal experience. The experience of the individual became in reality that of Israel. That is why it was preserved by the people in Bible and Prayer Book. And their point of view is entirely colored by an intense God-consciousness. They knew God and experienced Him intensely. They saw Him in nature, in history, in the daily affairs of men. They saw Him in the vast universe and they knew Him in their personal lives. And they sang of Him and His attributes, of His law and His truth, of His relation to Israel and to mankind and of our obligations toward Him. Their poetry breathes, therefore, with deep religious fervor and earnestness, with a moral passion and a loyalty that inspire us today as of old.

The best they wrote, through the Bible and Prayer Book, became the means of worship for the Jew, and the joy derived through prayer, the consolation and the inspiration which prayer and meditation gave them, have kept and preserved the Jew loyal and faithful to the finest and noblest elements of his ethics, of his faith, of his people and his history.

DECLARATION OF FAITH AND VOW

Tradition tells us that on this day, thousands of years ago, our forefathers stood at Mount Sinai and there, amidst thunder and lightning, they received the Ten Commandments, which have become the basis of all law. They received these laws with a fervor characteristic of the pioneer. They entered, then and there, into an everlasting covenant with God and accepted a law as a safeguard to the freedom they had just attained.

Today, we, the heirs of that past, are also entering into a covenant with God and with Israel. It is a covenant of faithfulness, a covenant whose keywords are: *"Na'aseh v'nishma,"* "We shall heed and we shall hear." This covenant imposes great obligations upon us, and we assume them joyously.

"But," you might ask, "what proof have you to offer that you are capable of assuming these obligations?" And our answer is simple. In the years of our religious school training, we have been taught the ideals of Judaism as found in the Bible and as interpreted by poets, philosophers, and teachers. Also, we have been given special instruction by our Rabbi for the past two years, in the principles of our faith. In addition, we have our willingness to learn more and our desire to be Jews by conviction as well as by birth. This training, our realization that we have just begun to learn, and our will to be loyal are both our proof and our promise that we shall meet our newer obligations in a manner that will do honor to ourselves, to you and to Judaism.

As that faithful band of Israelites stood and trembled in awe before Sinai, so we, with that same awe and expectation, are eager to make our vows. Standing on this sacred altar, before you, our parents; before you, our Rabbi, and you, the assembled congregation, fervently and hopefully, solemnly and earnestly we make this vow:

[*The Confirmands rise and recite in unison:*]

"I consecrate my life to my people and to my people's faith. With all my heart, with all my soul, and with all my might will I endeavor to further the lofty aims of Judaism and to practice the ideals of the Jew. Unto the end of my days Israel's watchword shall be the slogan of my life and that which it represents will be my guide and inspiration. *Sh'ma Yisroel, Adonoi Elohenu, Adonoi Echod.* Hear, O Israel, the Lord our God, the Lord is One."

Choir:

"Boruch Shem K'vod Malchuso L'olom Vo'ed."

(Praised be His name whose glorious Kingdom is for ever and ever.)

Hymn

Let Israel strive for truth alone,
    And in His power confide—
For He is faithful to His word
    If we in Him abide.
His councils must forever stand;
    All nations bow to His command.

Let Israel strive for truth alone
    In love to bless mankind,
And in the bonds of brotherhood
    All nations soon to bind;
So that they all, with one accord,
    Acknowledge and obey the Lord.

THE RABBI'S CONFIRMATION CHARGE

The Adventure of Judaism

My dear Boys and Girls:

It is given to me to know some things about you which even those most precious of all beings, your parents, may not know. I know something of your religious doubts; I know something of your thoughts and I also know much of the splendid spirit that is yours today. I rejoice in my knowledge of these as I rejoice in your spirit.

Today, you assume formally the responsibilities of Jewish life. What is it that we offer you when we offer you Judaism? Very definitely, it is not a path of ease. Very emphatically, it is not a sanction of loose living. Certainly, it is not a screen behind which you might hide.

Rather do we offer you, and you assume, the "Yoke of the Kingdom of Heaven." It is the "Yoke of the Commandments" that we place upon you. And as we offer these to you and you accept them, we invite you to set out upon a great adventure. Your point of departure is this synagogue. Your time of departure is this moment. The name of the vessel you set out upon is *The Spirit of Judaism*. Your destination is the Kingdom of God.

Our blessings accompany you. We, your parents and teachers, are thrilled and uplifted by this moment. We are literally lifted out of the humdrum of daily existence and eagerly with you we face the future, although, with you, too, we share the anxiety of the moment.

It is a tremendous adventure that is before you! We do not promise you fair weather; quite to the contrary, we assure you of storms and hardships. You will know of the cold—of misunderstanding. You will experience the sleet—of persecution. You will run into the fog—of hatred. You will fly over waters of destruction and through clouds of danger. And always, you will fly *alone*.

Oh, you will know of our prayers and anxiety and concern for you. These may help you, perhaps; these may cause you to feel less alone. Nevertheless, you will navigate alone; alone, that is, with God. After all, none can live for you, none can adventure for you. These must be done by yourselves.

The ship in which you will fly, *The Spirit of Judaism,* will make very definite demands upon you which will have to be satisfied or the ship will not function. It will need fuel and oil. It will require delicate adjustment and it will demand the complete coordination of all of its parts.

What are these?

May I suggest to you that your sense of loyalty is the fuel you require. That your devotion is to be the oil. That with self-respect you can make adjustment, and through self-restraint and discipline, you can effect the coordination of all of the parts. But note, this loyalty, this self-restraint, this devotion, this self-respect, this discipline—all of these spell *character,* and this *you* must bring to the enterprise.

But even this is not enough. More is required. You will remember that *The Spirit of St. Louis* without the spirit of Lindbergh on that great adventure of his across the Atlantic, would have been but junk. But, with Lindbergh, *The Spirit of St. Louis* became a graceful, animated vessel, doing that which people called impossible.

Remember this too: were Lindbergh a novice, he never could have risen from the ground. Before he attempted that epoch-making flight, there was a long period of training and with it, there was a consuming eagerness to fly; and that was stimulated and enhanced by his delight and joy over the possibility of achieving. His was the spirit of adventure, a spirit made up of daring and unostentatiousness. Possessed of these, Lindbergh ventured forth and the distance between Paris and New York was reduced to 33½ hours. And that which had never been done, now was done. That which people said cannot be done, Lindbergh demonstrated to be possible. But more than that: he demonstrated that it ought to be done. For the spirit of progress is the spirit of daring to overcome the impossible. Faith in the possibility of progress when coupled with trained application and discipline makes for achievement. You will remember that the trans-Atlantic cable was once considered an impossibility. You will remember that the telephone was deemed impossible. You will recall that the wireless and the radio and even aviation were deemed out of the range of human possibility.

Similarly, in the life of the spirit and ideals, slavery was once approved and its elimination was not to be thought of. But, it has been eliminated. No doubt, when democracy and self-government were first spoken of, there were those wise ones who said, "It won't work, it has never been done." But it did work and it has been done. When education for the masses was being urged, there were those cautious ones who said that popular education was dangerous, that people would not know how to make use of it. Well, someone dared to do it and it was done. People who urged these things were called fools. Some of them were persecuted. All of them were laughed at and scorned. "The prophet is a fool, the man of spirit is insane." That has been the cry that we have heard through the ages raised against those who nobly dared. But the time comes when the prophets are adulated even by the mobs who but a short time before disapproved.

What caused the change in the attitude of the mob? It was the persistence of those who knew what was right—of the men of faith and of daring. It was their perseverance. It was their patience and their confidence. Given these, the impossibility vanished, the fanciful became the essential, the foolish became the heroic, the foolhardy became the achievement. The fact that something had never been done does not mean that it ought not to be done or that it cannot be done. But this is certain. Things do not just happen. In each case, there was training, there was discipline, there was intelligence and there was dar· ing.

Take the ideals which you have been taught and which you have accepted. When we speak of Justice, there are those who will tell you, It has never been done. When we speak of restraint, there will be some who will say, It is not being done. Mention piety to some and with a smirk they will ask: Who indulges in it? Suggest selflessness, and the cynics will say: Who knows anything about it? For them, money—it is God. For them, greed—it is virtue, self-indulgence is worship.

To follow these, to be sure, is to swim with the current, and I confess that that is easy. But I caution you and warn you that such is not the way of *The Spirit of Judaism*. The way of Judaism, some will say, is impossible. I say to you, my boys and girls, it is possible! It has never been tried. And I urge you to try the Jewish way. Difficult it is? Yes! But you are young. And

> "When duty whispers low, 'Thou must!'
> The Youth replies, 'I can.'"

And with that reply, caution is sent into discard and adventure becomes a lure and a compulsion.

For daring and venturing some will call you fools. What of it? Do you know that you are right? If you do, that alone matters. Do not waver. Let others waver. You be the constant factors in life. Do you believe that ideals are worth having? If you do, then you should realize also that ideals are worth struggling for, are worth suffering for, are worth enduring for. Do you believe that Judaism is worth preserving? Then *you* must preserve it!

But how? you might ask. Let me refer to Lindbergh's flight

once again. In his ship, he had an instrument board. Those instruments had been tested. He learned how to use them, and, having learned, he did use them. And because they were tested and because he knew how to use them and did so, he succeeded in his attempt.

You, too, have your instruments to guide you and to direct you. There are instruments that come with *The Spirit of Judaism*. To be sure, they are symbolic but they are effective.

First, there is the Bible which you deposited in the shrine this morning. Let the Bible be your compass. Use it, know it, study it. You will always know how to bank and turn to keep afloat if you will know the direction that is right.

Second, you have brought your prayer book, which you also deposited in the Ark. I should say that this prayer book corresponds to the altimeter. It helps you to soar, to aspire, to reach unto the heights of heights.

Third, you have brought the symbol of human service. I should say that this corresponds to the earth inductor compass. It helps you to keep contact with earth, with practical life, with the problems and needs of men and women and children. It keeps you in contact with them all and prevents you from soaring away from them.

And then, you have brought a cluster of flowers with you. Six white rosebuds. Let me suggest that these buds represent the letters of the one word *Israel*.

Let the first one represent the letter *I* in the word *Innocence*. I will ask you to take this bud out of its cluster, and when you approach the shrine later to receive your blessing, that you deposit it there, to be preserved as a lasting testimony of your pledge made here today to lead a life of purity and innocence.

Let the second bud stand for the letter *S* to symbolize the word *Sacrifice*. I will ask you to give that flower to your parents. Ask them to preserve it as a token of your appreciation of and gratitude for the sacrifices they have made in your behalf. And let it be preserved by them as the assurance given by you this day that you will make sacrifices if need be to lead lives that will be useful and noble.

Let the third bud stand for the letter *R*. It symbolizes *Religion*. I will ask you to give that bud to me, your Rabbi. I shall preserve it as a token of your pledge to be always faithful and loyal to the religion that is ours.

The fourth bud represents the letter *A*. It stands for the word *Altruism*. Give this to some philanthropic institution. Ask the custodian to preserve it as a lasting testimony of your sacred promise made today to live for others and to make the lives of others brighter, happier and more cheerful.

The fifth bud, representing the letter *E,* symbolizes *Education*. Give that bud to one of your teachers and ask her to preserve it as a pledge made by you faithfully to pursue the quest after knowledge.

The sixth bud represents the letter *L* and the word *Labor*. Preserve that one yourselves and let it ever be a reminder to you of the pledge you have given to consecrate your lives to honorable and useful labor for the good of mankind.

These are the ingredients of the fuel which will help keep your vessel aloft. And these, with your loyalty, with your training and your devotion will make it possible for you to navigate the good ship, *The Spirit of Judaism*.

You have deposited these symbols in the Ark. I shall now return them to you, and as I give them back to you, I give you also this slogan, *"Derech emunah bacharti"*—"I have chosen the way of faithfulness" (Ps. 119:30). Take them, use them, dare greatly, soar nobly, achieve honorably.

In God's name then, come!

[*At the conclusion of the charge the emblems deposited in the Ark are returned. When the children return to their seats the Congregation unites in singing the following hymn.*]

HYMN

Witness, ye men and women, now
  Before the Lord we speak;
To Him we make our solemn vow
  With hearts devout and meek.

That, long as life itself shall last,
  Ourselves to God we yield,
That from His cause we'll ne'er depart,
  To whom our vows are sealed.

Lord, guide our faltering feet aright,
  And keep us in Thy ways,
And while we turn our vows to prayers
  Turn Thou our prayers to praise.

OUR GRATITUDE

We, Confirmands, shall not endeavor to express in words that are adequate that appreciation with which our hearts are overflowing. Up to this turning point in our lives, we have been watched over untiringly by you, dear parents, teachers and congregation.

You, our parents, have shown us, from our infancy, the difference between right and wrong; you have given us every opportunity in your power to become educated in the history and faith of our ancestors. The homes you have established have protected us from the trials and dangers of the world outside. And if we needed homes up to now, if we needed your guidance and counsel heretofor, how much the more shall we need those in the days and years to come, as we go through, probably, the most difficult and dangerous period of our lives? And so, we assure you, dear parents, of our appreciation, and pledge to you to do our utmost from now on to repay you in love, in honor, in faithfulness the debt we owe you.

Under our Rabbi's guidance and with our teachers we have studied the beliefs of our fathers and the history of our people. Our teachers have inspired us to higher ideals through the example they set. Our dear Rabbi has been our friend and adviser, patient and eager to help and guide us personally. We appreciate these. But again, we mean to prove our gratitude by the lives we shall lead, by the service we shall render, by continuing to study Jewish life and literature, by accepting the guidance and following the leadership of our Rabbi.

And so, to you, members of this historic Jewish congregation, who have given us School and Synagogue, teachers and Rabbi, who have urged us and challenged us to be loyally Jewish, to *live* as Jews rather than just *talk* as Jews, we, the future congregation speak our gratitude and promise that we shall earnestly continue and, wherever possible, better the work which you have done and the service you rendered to the Jewish and general community.

BLESSING THE CONFIRMANDS—THE RABBI

CLOSING PRAYER

OUR GOD AND FATHER:

As we stand on the threshold of the life of responsibility that lies before us, in this solemn hour, on this day of our consecration, we, Thy children, realize full well the greatness of the task ahead of us, and our hearts tremble with awe and fear. Unto us a sacred charge has this day been committed. Into our keeping a people's destiny and our people's hopes have been entrusted. Will we be faithful to the charge? Will we be equal to the task? We peer wonderingly into the future and out of the depths of our anxiety, out of the deepest recesses of our hearts we pray: Help us, O Thou, Guardian of Israel! Keep us worthy of this day! Help us to remain strong in resolution, earnest and sincere and reverent as we are this day. Guide our footsteps that we may avoid the pitfalls of life! Give us wisdom and strength to overcome any obstacles that may beset our paths. May we grow up firm and steadfast of purpose and pure and upright of character. In all our ways may we ever know Thee. From Thee and Thy ways may we learn to be ever generous in thought and deed, helpful unto others and considerate of all, so that in our lives and through them there may be reflected our never failing love of Thee and Thy truth.

May the words of our mouths and the meditations of our hearts be acceptable in Thy sight, our Rock and our Redeemer. Amen.

Hymn

Suppliant low, Thy children bend,
   Father, for Thy blessing now;
Thou canst teach us, guide, defend;
   We are weak, almighty Thou.

With the peace Thy word imparts
   Be the taught and teachers blest;
In our lives and in our hearts,
   Father, be Thy laws impressed.

Grant us spirits lowly, pure,
   Errors pardoned, sins forgiven,
Humble trust, obedience sure,
   Love to man, and faith in Heaven.

CONCLUDING SERVICE
(Union Prayer Book, page 272)

RECESSIONAL

[*Congregation and Confirmands singing as concluding Hymn,*]
"En Kelohenu"

BENEDICTION

ORGAN POSTLUDE

Confirmation Service

II

Organ Prelude

SHABUOTH SERVICE
(Union Prayer Book, pages 206-220, 229, 238)

Processional (Organ)—"Coronation March"......*Meyerbeer*

[*Escorted by Confirmands of other years and led by Officials of the Congregation, the Confirmands enter the Temple, each bearing a Bible, a Prayer Book, Six White Rosebuds, and an Emblem of Human Service. The Congregation is requested not to rise during the Processional.*]

Choir:

How blessèd are, how blessèd are who come in the name of the Lord, our God!

Oh, bless'd be ye, oh, bless'd be ye, in the house of the Lord our God.

How blessèd are, who come in the name of the Lord our God!

Oh, bless'd be ye, in the house of the Lord our God.

OPENING PRAYER

Heavenly Father:

We stand before Thee with trembling hearts and reverent, awe-struck souls. More than ever before do we realize that we need Thee and love Thee. Therefore, we pray unto Thee. Help us to make this Confirmation Day a Day of Consecration, and the beginning of this Service the beginning of the continuous dedication of our lives to Thee and to Thy service, to Israel, to our country, and to mankind. Help us to make our glorious heritage even more glorious and more precious. We have received it as a body of high ideals, and noble precepts. Oh God, may our lives henceforth prove our gratefulness in our every act and thought so that we may hand down that which we received unsullied by any deed of ours or by failure on our part.

God of our fathers, how can we, inexperienced as we are, inadequate as is our speech, hope to show by pledges and vows how great is our gratitude for the loving, guiding parents with whom we are blessed? They have directed our lives into the channel of righteousness and have taught us to cling tenaciously to our faith. We thank Thee for them, even as we are thankful for our dear Rabbi and for members of our Congregation, our families and friends, who have given us a clearer understanding of Judaism and have set before us a true standard by which to live. May these gifts strengthen us to further Thy will and help us to attain a wholesome, tranquil life.

We seek Thy forgiveness, dear Lord, for our past transgressions, and at the same time ask that in Thy great goodness thou mayest pardon others who in past years have stood at the altar of Confirmation and have forgotten.

Guide us and all other confirmands, who are today declaring our faith, to a deeper and fuller realization of Thy Providence. May all assembled here, ever feel the yearning for Thy presence and seek the joy of communion with Thee. Help us at all times willingly to submit to Thy will thereby intensifying our faith and trust in Thee and in Thy wise dispensations. Amen.

A child in solving a puzzle is enthralled with it at first. But when the child has finally solved the puzzle, his interest in it begins to lag and he begins to seek another plaything. So, too, with people. Ever needing and seeking God, when they discovered the true character and inferiority of idols and their own superior strength and grasp on life, the old idolatries began to disappear, and they sought a God greater than they were and also one not circumscribed by environment.

Amongst all peoples some sort of God-idea is found. But it was our ancestors who *first* began to speak of and worship one God, the God of all the universe, the God of all mankind. It was they who first spoke of Him as spiritual rather than material, as ethical rather than selfish, as the Intelligence informing life, as a benevolent Providence manifest throughout, as the One who gives purpose and significance to life. From the lower idea of God to the highest our people adventured until they came to the ideal of a God who demands justice and righteousness, a God who is greater than life and yet part of it.

We deposited our Bibles in the sacred Ark today in token of our recognition of the existence of this Source of all being, of this Cause of all life, of this Ideal of Perfection, the Reality whom we call God. We deposited our Bibles in token of our pledge to continue the search after God, to seek to attain unto an ever expanding idea of Him, to continue to grow and to develop with that idea, so to live that by our deeds and our lives we may demonstrate not alone our faith in Him, but reveal Him as an ever-present, loving and moral influence upon our lives.

ISRAEL

The Bible is in a very significant sense Israel's book. It has even been designated by some as "the spiritual autobiography of the Jew." It reveals Israel's spiritual growth through the presentation of the history of the Jew, of his poetry and drama, of the wisdom of his sages and the impassioned utterances of his prophets. From beginning to end we have a record of Israel's spiritual ascendency and always is the material and physical aspect of history used as a means to indicate the spiritual, the moral development of our people.

Thus we have in the Bible not alone the theme of God in life, but also of Israel as an agent in the divine economy of life. Israel is represented to be not as the pet, the darling of God upon whom He would shower all of the choicest material blessings and comforts. Israel is conceived to be the first born in the household of the spirit, in the sanctuary of pure faith. Israel is thought of as the living witness to a living yet invisible and incorporeal God. Israel does not consider himself an aristocracy in the social and lower sense, but rather " a kingdom of priests and a holy people." In other words, a *spiritual* aristocracy, a people dedicated to and consecrated by an ideal of service. Israel becomes therefore the servant of the Lord, even the suffering servant of the Lord, the "despised, and forsaken of men, a man of pains and acquainted with disease, and as one from whom men hide their face." Israel is believed to be the messenger of a great truth rather than the claimant of special recognition; the emissary of ethical, spiritual idealism, the monitor of religious truth.

We deposited our Bibles in the Ark in token of our pledge that we mean to be worthy of the heritage which is our people's. We recognize that ours is the duty to be worthy of the spiritual nobility transmitted to us and we recognize our obligations which today we consciously assume to continue faithful to the mission which is our people's, to continue loyal to the task which is ours as Jews, to continue devoted members and faithful servants in the ranks of the priestly people, servants and ministers of the Ideal.

MANKIND

The Bible speaks not alone of God and Israel, but also of Mankind. The Rabbis of old recognized and stressed this fact. There is an account in the Talmud of the great Rabbis Akiba and Ben Zoma trying to discover the greatest sentence in the Bible. Rabbi Akiba said that it was "Love thy neighbor as thyself." Ben Zoma disagreed, saying that in his opinion, the words in Genesis "This is the Book of the generations of *man*" was the greatest sentence. Both recognized mankind as the most important factor with whom God concerns Himself. Not one race or another, not one people or another, but man, mankind, humanity, is the goal of the religious law. Indeed, the Rabbis said that the reason that the Ten Commandments were given on the lonely mountain in the wilderness, in No Man's Land, so to speak, was, that no one people could claim that the moral law applies only to one group.

And so, too, as we turn the pages of the Bible we find again and again an emphasis upon the dignity of man and human personality that is quite unique. In the Book of Jonah, or the Book of Ruth, in the Bible, this idea is especially stressed and spiritual glory or the possibility of it is ascribed to all peoples who walk in the path of the Lord. It was the Psalmist who speaks of *man,* not alone Israel, whom God has made but little lower than the angels and crowned him with glory and honor.

Again, it was the Prophet Malachi who asked, "Have we not all one Father? Hath not one God created us all? Why then should we deal treacherously a man with his brother?" And still again we find in the Proverbs the idea that the soul of *man* regardless of race, creed, origin, environment, the soul of *man* is the light of the Lord. Many other passages might be quoted to demonstrate the insistence of Israel's seekers upon the human element, and their repeated stress upon the dignity of man. Out of such stress and emphasis are the ideas of human brotherhood, of friendship and human fellowship born, and a sacredness is ascribed to these which challenges the best efforts of all men everywhere to live peacefully and cooperatively together and through common endeavor to seek to realize the greatest hopes and ideals of which the mind of man is capable.

And so, as we deposit our Bible in the Ark, it is in token of our pledge that having been taught to think in terms of mankind, having been led to believe that men are brothers, having been guided to recognize the dignity and value of human personality, we shall attempt to give our best efforts to the task of fulfilling this ideal and achieving this task.

THE PRAYER BOOK OFFERING

REVERENCE

We have deposited in the Ark also our Prayer Book, and the Prayer Book suggests the importance of reverence in life. For the Prayer Book reminds us that we, by ourselves and unto ourselves, are not sufficient. We are dependent on Higher Will and Power. We are dependent upon that Other of whose will and purpose we are but tools and instruments. This realization must bring to us an attitude of the deepest respect, a recognition of the sacredness of all life and leads one to a sense of reverence.

What is reverence? Some think it is but a gesture, a bowed head, quiet bearing, a hush of silence. These are but the externals of reverence. The dictionary correctly defines reverence as a deep respect, accompanied by a feeling of awe and affection. Reverence, therefore, is more than a gesture. It is a deep-seated emotion, something that comes from within. And as we realize our human insufficiency and as we become aware of the greater Presence and sanctity outside of us, there comes the sense of awe which goes over into respect touched with love.

And so the Prayer Book tells us of reverence to God, but really it goes beyond that. We should be reverent in the presence of all and toward all, man and experience alike, which leads us to think of all that is good and true, beautiful and noble. Thus reverence is due to our parents, to our teachers, the good and noble men and women everywhere. Reverence is due to great ideals and great thoughts and hopes. Reverence is due to institutions which are symbols of the great ideals of man. Reverence is due to our own persons and personalities because we are created in the spiritual likeness of God. And reverence may be expressed by our lives and deeds, by our attitude and bearing, by our speech and our thoughts.

This duty to be reverent we have been taught. We are convinced of its truth and importance. We pledge ourselves to be reverent, to be respectful, and to live as if we were always in the house of God, ever in the presence of our Maker.

WORSHIP AND PRAYER

From reverence to worship is but a step, and certainly the Prayer Book speaks to us of that communion which men have ever sought and ever had with God. People worshipped and still worship in many and diverse ways. But essentially, prayer and worship are means of expression of the purest and noblest emotions within us and communication of these to the God of life. Such communion may be our voicing of thanks to God for the manifold blessings which are ours, such as parents, friends, health, strength, home, comforts, education, and gratitude for His revelation of Himself to us.

This communion with God may take the form of adoration and praise, just awe expressed in words or attitude, adoration of God who established the harmony of the universe.

This communion may take the form of confession which comes from our recognition of failure to live up to the highest ideals of which we are capable. We may come before Him with petitions when we communicate to Him our desires and our hopes, though we should ever be careful to ask *not for things,* but for spiritual guidance and inspiration.

People have often tried to analyze prayer. They have tried to find the psychology of prayer, they have tried to discover whether prayer is answered or not; and yet man prays despite all. It is part of his nature to worship and to pray. Man prays in all environments and in all moods; man prays alone, and man raises his voice in prayer in the midst of an assembly of men. Man prays spontaneously and voluntarily, and again, he speaks the words which have poured forth from the believing soul of another and finds joy and satisfaction in repeating the words.

And so we recognize the importance, the need and value of worship. We recognize the satisfaction and the help that come through it. Therefore we brought our Prayer Books with us here on this Day of Consecration, and as we give ourselves in earnestness and sincerity to the higher life, we deposited our Prayer Books in the Ark in token of our pledge sincerely and earnestly to commune with God, to unburden our souls before Him, reverently to speak our needs and earnestly to try to be near unto Him as He is near unto all who call upon Him, who call upon Him in truth.

THE SYNAGOGUE

As the Prayer Book tells us of worship and reverence, it does also speak to us of the Synagogue, that unique institution created by the Jew for his religious, spiritual, educational and communal purposes.

The Synagogue originated some 2500 years ago in Babylon as the rallying point of the Jewish community in dispersion. It was the meeting place of worshipper, teacher, pupil, the people generally. And since that day, through the many centuries, and especially since the final destruction of the Temple in the year 70, the Synagogue became the rallying point of the dispersed and scattered people, and in a very real sense, the conserver of Jewish values, as indeed of Jewish life. Whether the Jew would have survived these many centuries without the Synagogue is problematical, for it was in the Synagogue that hope was fanned into being; it was here that faith was instilled to keep the drooping spirit buoyant; it was here that the Jewish soul found solace and comfort and inspiration.

And the modern Synagogue, like unto its forerunners in the past, is at the heart of Jewish life. It makes for continuity, the continuity of people and faith. It continues the free interpretation of the traditions and history of our people. Through its religious school, it instructs the young; through its pulpit, it seeks to educate the adult; it is concerned with the past, but it is part of the cultural background of the present, and in the light of its interpretation, its point of view, its idealism, modern problems are judged in a perspective that is helpful. The Synagogue, too, is the means through which the message of Judaism is given to the world.

Into the Synagogue we today are formally admitted. Part of its spirit is given to us, and the challenge of its service we are called upon to accept. To the Synagogue, therefore, we give ourselves today. Its worship shall help us, its message shall enlighten us, and we in turn, by our lives and loyalty, shall strengthen it and maintain it as the hub of modern Jewish experience.

HYMN

Father of Life and Light and Pow'r,
To Thee we consecrate this hour!
With earnest hope, with purpose pure,
O make this happy promise sure.

Help us to lay foundations strong
Of love for right, of grief for wrong;
And brotherhood with every race
That seeks or needs the Father's grace.

Help us to grow in pure desires,
Kindle our souls with heavenly fires,
That higher levels may be won
And step by step Thy will be done.

Build in us all Thy spirit's shrine,
Then shall we beam with light divine,
"And work with heart and soul and might
For Truth and Freedom, God and Right."

THE FLOWER OFFERING

THE BEAUTY OF HOLINESS

The flower suggests innocence, purity, flawlessness and above all beauty. Take, for instance, a rosebud. When we look at it we feel that it is a sacred thing, it speaks to us of God, it suggests holiness. It is a symbol of both beauty and holiness, and tells us of the beauty of holiness.

In the past, and among primitive people even today, holiness is synonymous with taboo, and anything that is taboo must not be used or even touched. In other words, taboo is uselessness in the name of holiness. The Jewish idea, as taught by the prophets and sages, is different. Holiness to the Jew means moral perfection, and moral perfection means usefulness, goodness, justice and righteousness.

Holiness, therefore, means spiritual and moral beauty. Take the Ten Commandments as an example. We are bidden: Do not steal; do not commit adultery; do not murder. These are not alone prohibitions. They tell us also to be honest, they tell us to be clean and to lead pure lives. They tell us to cherish life and health and to preserve them; not alone our own lives, but also those of all other men, women and children. This it is to lead sacred, holy lives, and such lives are noble and beautiful.

We are bidden to honor our parents; to remember and observe the Sabbath; not to bear false witness against our neighbors. Helping others, showing loving kindness to others, being gracious, reverent, unselfish—all this is holiness and in that there is beauty. For sin is ugly, wrong doing is ugly, corruption is ugly, uselessness is unattractive, selfishness is hideous.

"Holy shall ye be, because I, the Lord your God, am holy." This sums up the whole matter. And in such holiness, in such moral living, in purity and service there is that which makes life beautiful and living a joy and a blessing. And so, as we deposit our rosebuds in the Sanctuary, we pledge ourselves to lead lives that will demonstrate to all the beauty that is holiness.

THE FRAGRANCE OF CHARACTER

To what can character be more truly compared than to the rosebuds which we deposited in the sacred Ark? Their fragrance is not something that comes from without; it is part of their very essence, natural as their color is, real as is their beauty. So, too, is character. It is not good character when it is artificial. It must be the revelation of the very essence of man, and must be natural, and unassumed. Someone said, that true character is that which a man is when no one is looking, and such character when it is good is fragrant and wholesome. It is true, also, that the fragrance of the flower radiates all about it, and settles upon all that comes in contact with it. So, too, is good character. It is contagious. It expands the heart and soul of the possessor not only; it challenges and strengthens as it touches the characters of others.

But more than that. To be of good character is to earn the esteem and respect of others. It is to possess a good reputation, a "good name," the noblest possession we can have. One of Israel's sages once said: "There are three crowns, the crown of Torah, the crown of priesthood, and the crown of royalty; but the crown of a good name excells them all." Wealth without a good name, power without good character, position and influence when not founded on goodness, merit, or virtue, may last for a while, but are worthless when judged by eternal standards. "A good name is rather to be chosen than great riches, and esteem is more than money" or power or caste. For goodness is like the fragrance of the rose. It is a distinction to him who has it; it blesses all who come in contact with it.

And thus, as we deposit the fragrant buds in the sacred Ark we mean it to be our pledge to cultivate good character, to seek to earn the esteem of mankind, to be deserving of the diadem of a good name.

THE ETERNITY OF LIFE

A world without flowers! Picture it! What a drab world it would be! For a flower is the symbol of beauty, of fragrance; indeed, of life. It is the token of the continuity of life, of man never-dying. The flower withers, to be sure. Yet ere a twelvemonth passes it blooms in glory reborn. Resurrected anew each year, it never *really* dies.

So with mankind. We do not *really* die. What we call "death" is but a transition, a change, a going forth *from* life *to* life. It is an interlude in the eternal drama of life.

> "Dust thou art to dust returnest,
> Was not spoken of the soul."

For the soul, a spark of God's divine essence, does not perish, though the body wither and decay. Man lives on, in the hearts of those dear to him, in the influences radiated, in the deeds performed, in the lingering memories of those who cannot forget. Man lives on because, as a Jewish teacher phrased it: "We are in the stream of life and we cannot escape it. Our life began with the life of the universe and can only end with it. . . . Death is the peak of a life-wave, and so is birth. Death and birth are one."

To be sure, we do not know what the next stage of life for us may be. We know nothing of the hereafter. But this we know, God *is*. "His universe is perfect and our destiny is part of His perfection." The rest matters little. "Even though I walk through the valley of the shadow of death, I will fear no evil for *Thou* art with me. . . . I dwell in the house of the Lord forever."

In our Prayer Book, in the Memorial Ritual for the Day of Atonement, I found a beautiful poem which reads in part:

> "Why art thou cast down, my soul?
> Why disquieted in me?
> Lo, thy dead live on immortal!
> For God's messenger of love
> Them hath guided through death's portal
> To the larger life above."

From life to life—this is the fact. "Hostages to eternity"—
these are our dead, even we, alive today. "Death is swallowed
up in Eternity." And because life is continuous, because it is
never ending, because it is eternal, *there are no dead!*

THE SYMBOL OF SERVICE

Our Debt to Society

Into the Ark we have this day deposited, along with the
Bible, the Prayer Book, and the rosebuds, a simple pin shaped
in the form of the six-pointed star of the Synagogue, the
Mogen Dovid, upon which the word "Service" is inscribed.
This symbol of humane service is a token of our recognition
that man never lives by himself, that we are born into a society and we live our lives in the midst of, and in contact with
others. In such life and contacts there are blessings and privi-
leges, but there are also definite and binding duties. We bene-
fit by the lives and deeds of others. Others must be enriched
and made happy by our lives and deeds and service.

We owe it to society, specifically to make it possible for
others to live full and rounded lives. We owe it to society to
make every effort to assure to all others *that* life, liberty, and
happiness which we seek and crave ourselves. It is our duty
so to live and so to influence life that all men may have the
opportunity to earn a livelihood, to educate themselves and to
educate their children, to enjoy the blessings of nature and
cultural opportunities, to give friendship and fellowship to
others even as we crave them for ourselves. These we should
give to others not because we do not need them but just
because we need them; not because we are prepared to
discard these, but because it is the just due of others to have
these.

We owe it to society to share our lives with others and, more especially, is it our duty to help those who are underprivileged and have not the means to enjoy the simple blessings of life to which, as human beings, they are entitled. If we are blessed with knowledge, others should be the wiser for it; if we are blessed with strength, others should be the stronger; if with wealth, others should be the happier.

The late Nathan Straus, lover of men, had this sense of responsibility for others to a noble degree. In his will was found the following passage:

"I have always been deeply impressed by an old Jewish proverb which says: 'What you give for the cause of charity in health is gold; what you give in sickness is silver; what you give after death is lead!'"

This old proverb by which Nathan Straus guided his life is one by which all of us might guide ours, for it speaks of responsibility and duty, it speaks of sharing life with others, it speaks of the joy and happiness of service.

We, the Confirmands, have been taught these duties and earnestly hope to be able to fulfill our duties to society. We resolve earnestly to be helpful to all men and women, who earnestly and sincerely strive to make this a better world, and who seek to establish here such justice and such righteousness as shall be based upon genuine cooperation and if need be, sacrificial service.

Peace and Goodwill

Not long ago, while in New York, I saw in the Metropolitan Museum of Art a statue by Butensky. At the base of this statue are the figures of a lion and a lamb, the great and the small, the strong and the weak, the aggressor and the meek, lying peacefully side by side. Behind an anvil stands a man, the prophet Isaiah, with one arm uplifted, holding a mallet. The other arm is holding a bundle of swords, which have been beaten until they begin to take the form of a ploughshare. And on the base of this statue one reads the one Hebrew word, *"Shalom"*—"Peace."

The sculptor here represents the age-old ideal of the Jew, his hope and dream—Universal Peace. Peace is not only one of the central ideals of Jewish life, but it is conceived to be Israel's mission in life.

But, there can be no peace without goodwill. For before there is peace there must be demobilization of hatred, of mistrust, of suspicion, of ill-will. First there must be the realization that men are brothers, and respect and affection must rule our conduct toward each other. Peace and goodwill are, therefore, each dependent upon the other.

And then, too, to have peace we must want it, honor it, seek it and pursue it. When we shall remember to honor the heroes of peace, even more than we honor the heroes of war; when we shall sing the praises of those who preserve life, rather than of those who destroy it; when we shall use science to bless, rather than to curse humanity; when we shall use art to glorify peace, rather than to idealize war; when poets shall sing hymns of human fellowship, rather than hymns of hate; when patriotism will begin to be understood in the light of respect for the preservation of the homes of others because we love *our* homes, and wish others to respect them; when we shall follow the golden rule of Hillel, "What is hateful unto thee, that do not unto thy neighbor"—then we shall have peace, for then, in the words of Isaiah, "nation shall not lift up sword against nation, because they shall learn war no more."

In token of this resolution have we deposited in the sanctuary the symbol of Human Service and later as we wear it, it will serve as a reminder to us of our pledge here made to seek the ways of pleasantness and to pursue the paths of peace.

DECLARATION OF FAITH AND VOW

We are here today to be confirmed. But we would not be here, had we not already been confirmed. We have been going through the process of confirmation over a period of years. We are here less to be validated by formal assent, but more to be given and to give a newer assurance of the reality of those ideals in the truth of which we have already been confirmed.

There is a beautiful legend told by our ancient sages. They said that when the Israelites stood before Mount Sinai to receive the Law, the Lord said to them: "If I should give you the Law, what good sureties can you bring me to vouch for you that you will guard it?" The Israelites answered: "Our ancestors will vouch for us!" But the Lord said: "Oh no, your ancestors need sureties themselves." Then the Israelites said: "Our Prophets will vouch for us." But the Lord said: "Your Prophets are not sufficient." Then the Israelites exclaimed: "Our children will be our sureties." And the Lord said: "These are certainly good sureties and on their account I will give you the Law."

We, today, are the sureties for the validity and security of the moral law and of the moral life. We are going forth today to confirm the pledges of our forefathers. We, in our class, have studied and analyzed and discussed the Ten Commandments, and are convinced that the ideals taught by them are the fundamental ideals of Judaism, in fact the fundamental ideals of mankind. It is these ideals which we make our own and which we are going forth to confirm and strengthen, not by our words alone, but by the deeds of our lives, as well.

My classmates have spoken of those other aspects of Jewish teaching and doctrine which are central to Jewish life. They have spoken of God, the noblest ideal; of Israel—His servant; of mankind—His concern. They have spoken of the importance of Reverence and of the value of Worship; of loyalty to the Synagogue and service through it. They spoke of holiness and its beauty, of character and its fragrance, of the everlasting-ness of life. They spoke of duties to God and duties to man, of peace and good will among men. Each spoke not for him-self or herself alone, but for all of us. Those are the ideals to which we consecrate ourselves, those are the truths we con-firm. It is these obligations that we assume as in this house of God, at this altar of consecration, invoking memories that are sweet and sacred, in the presence of loved ones and dear ones, before God and in the Congregation of the faithful we now rise and declare our faith and make our vow:

[*The Confirmands rise and recite in unison:*]

"I consecrate my life to my people and to my people's faith. With all my heart, with all my soul, and with all my might will I endeavor to further the lofty aims of Judaism and to practise the ideals of the Jew. Unto the end of my days Israel's watchword shall be the slogan of my life and that which it represents will be my guide and inspiration. *Sh'ma Yisroel, Adonoi Elohenu, Adonoi Echod.* Hear, O Israel, the Lord our God, the Lord is One."

CHOIR:

"Boruch Shem K'vod Malchuso L'olom Vo'ed"
(Praised be His name whose glorious Kingdom is forever and ever)

HYMN

Witness, ye men and women, now
  Before the Lord we speak;
To Him we make our solemn vow
  With hearts devout and meek.

That, long as life itself shall last,
Ourselves to God we yield,
That from His cause we'll ne'er depart,
To whom our vows are sealed.

Lord, guide our faltering feet aright,
And keep us in Thy ways,
And while we turn our vows to prayers
Turn Thou our prayers to praise.

THE RABBI'S CONFIRMATION CHARGE

THE SECOND BIRTH

In the Sanskrit language (which is the literary language of India), according to the poet Tagore, the bird is described as "twice born"—once in its limited shell and then in the freedom of the unbounded sky.

In Jewish life and tradition, the young boy before he became a Bar Mitzvah, had some religious duties but these were under his father's responsibility. That was the shell stage. His freedom was limited because he had no responsibility. But when he attained the dignity of a Bar Mitzvah, or as we would say today, when he reached his confirmation, the responsibility for religious living became his own, and in the sphere of moral and religious responsibility, his was the freedom of the unbounded sky. This was the "second birth."

You, my dear pupils, have been brought here today, with what hopes you cannot yet understand. This day, we are placing upon you responsibility and with it, freedom. You are coming unto a second birth. You are just expanding your wings, so to speak. And before you fly away, mine is the privilege of charging you as to the future. I do so with a sense of responsibility that is eased by the consciousness of joy. And so I charge you to realize the beauty, the dignity, the necessity of using your wings now that you have attained unto your second birth. I charge you—do not be groundbirds, but soar and wing your way unto the heights. Keep your contact with the earth but do not dwell there exclusively. I charge you— into the air, into the clear air of ideals, into the very rays of the sun of righteousness, fly with a mighty effort and with a graceful motion. I charge you—rise above the limited, the circumscribed in the valley below, and above the crags and cliffs of life's elevations, soar and wing your way.

What do I mean by all this?

Just this:

Knowing life as I do, I know that the temptation is exceedingly great for all of us and any of us to take the line of least resistance. It is the easiest thing to do as others do; to agree with others, to let others think for us, to live from day to day only, to eat, drink, earn a livelihood, perform the routine tasks of life in a routine way and to be utterly and entirely smug and content. I admit that such an existence does have some compensations. But, oh, it is drab. It is uninteresting, it is uneventful, it is colorless.

There is another way and this is it. Perform your accepted tasks, do your duties, be they great or small, earn your livelihood honorably, enjoy your social contacts with your fellow humans; but do not pause there. Be not content with these; never, never become smug. Even in the midst of the usual, I bid you to live lives that will reach out mentally, spiritually beyond the commonplace. Seek out the principles of living. See yourselves, not alone in your immediate circle, but in relation to the larger world—indeed in relation to the universe. See yourselves as tools of deity, tools and agencies through whom God works, through whom God creates, through whom God fashions life. See yourselves as torch bearers, carrying the light of divine ideals into the very midst of the humdrum, the usual, even the sordid. When you think of yourselves in this way, you will discover that you will never be content with the physical alone. And such discontent is commendable, is desirable. I wish it for you.

I want you to see yourselves in relation to your fellow-beings, too. They long for happiness; help them to be happy. They yearn for peace; help them to realize it. They crave for life, the life abundant; help them to live it fully. They need dreams and visions, to give beauty to the everyday. Be ye the dreamers and the interpreters of daring dreams, the visionaries of ultimate goals. They need kindness and mercy; cultivate these for yourselves and for them. Do these and you will see and know life. You will see it whole and you will see it from the heights.

This, my dear young friends, is my advice to you on this your great day of your second birth. You do know the higher values of life. I have taught them to you. You have been informed of them. I charge you, do not forget them.

In a while, you will go hence from this sacred shrine and you will bear with you these symbols which today you brought here and deposited in the Ark.

Your Bible—let it be your *magna charta,* the charter of your spiritual freedom, the code by which your moral life is to be lived.

Your prayer book—let it be the symbol of your relationship to God, of your effort to reach unto communion with Him.

Your pin, the symbol of human service—let it be the re-minder of your duty to your neighbor, your fellow-man.

Your white rosebuds, six of them, standing for the six letters in the great name of *Israel*—let the first one, representing the letter *I* and the word *Innocence,* be deposited by you in this shrine today, as you approach it to receive your blessing. Let it be your solemn pledge to preserve the innocence and purity of your character.

Let the second, standing for the letter *S* and the word *Sacrifice,* be given by you to your parents in token for your gratitude for and in appreciation of the sacrifices they have made in rearing you and living for you.

Let the third flower, standing for the letter *R* and the word *Religion,* be given by you to me, your Rabbi, in token of your pledge that religion will be preserved by you, a meaningful and challenging experience of life.

Let the fourth rosebud, representing the letter *A* and the word *Altruism,* be given by you to some philanthropic agency to be preserved by them in token of your pledge given this day to live not for self alone but to strive to make the lives of others happier, more meaningful, more beautiful.

Let the next rosebud represent the letter *E* and the word *Education.* Give that to one of your teachers. Ask her to preserve it as a token of your pledge to keep your mind ever alert, to learn continuously, to be forever inquisitive.

Finally, let the remaining bud, standing for the letter *L* and the word *Labor,* be kept by you, and from time to time take it out, look at it, dream over it, and be reinspired to a life of effort in behalf of ideals.

These are Jewish ideals which are represented by the concepts I have spoken of. It is the Jewish bouquet. All of these symbols, I now return to you from the shrine where they have been hallowed. Come then unto me, my boys and girls, receive them at my hands, and go forth unto your second birth and to the freedom of unbounded service led on by ideals and visions!

[*At the conclusion of the charge the emblems deposited in the Ark are returned. When the children return to their seats, the Congregation unites in singing the following hymn.*]

HYMN

Suppliant low, Thy children bend
　　Father, for Thy blessing now;
Thou canst teach us, guide, defend:
　　We are weak, almighty Thou.

With the peace Thy word imparts
　　Be the taught and teachers blest;
In our lives and in our hearts,
　　Father, be Thy laws impressed.

Grant us spirits lowly, pure,
　　Errors pardoned, sins forgiven,
Humble trust, obedience sure,
　　Love to man, and faith in Heaven.

BLESSING THE CONFIRMANDS—THE RABBI

CLOSING PRAYER

But a few minutes more and we shall have concluded the
exercises of our Confirmation. We shall go forth from this
sacred altar with hearts deeply stirred, rejoicing yet anxious
concerning the promises given and the temptations which may
be found on the open road of life that stretches before us.

Today we have made a vow and given a pledge. May we
never fail in our sincerity and determination to fulfil them.
Help us to be worthy even of ourselves as we are today, and
may the thoughts that we now have in our minds, thoughts
of loyalty, of purity, of devotion, never leave us or be dismissed
by us. Grant, O Father, that we may find the courage to fulfill
our promises, and to abstain from such temptations as may
lead us into error and sin.

The religion which we have been taught and which we accepted this day has been the glory of many in the past. Grant then, dear God, that as we share this religion with them we may even enhance its beauty and brighten its glory through our lives.

In the history of our people heroic lives have kept the light of Judaism brightly burning. May the example of the past inspire us, too, as we continue, by Thy grace, the tradition of Jewish devotion and spiritual living.

Favor us, O Lord, by bestowing upon us the nature to be diligent in obedience to Thy word, to trust in Thee always, to confide in Thee continually, and to know Thee truly.

"May the words of our mouths and the meditations of our hearts be acceptable in thy sight O Lord, our Strength and our Redeemer." Amen.

Hymn

Lord, before Thy sacred Altar
　At the Temple's holy shrine,
Come Thy children with devotion
　To beseech Thy grace divine.
Here we pledge our consecration
　To the Law Thou didst reveal.
O may nations all revere it
　As life's holiest ideal.

O confirm our faith's devotion,
　To Thy sacred Law of truth;
To the vow our fathers rendered
　In our people's early youth.
So we vow, in faith enduring,
　To be steadfast to the trust,
Which at Sinai they accepted,
　Which accept we will and must.

And while men in great contention
   Still withhold to sing Thy praise,
May Thine ancient faithful people,
   Lead the nations in Thy ways.
As our fathers greatly suffering,
   Gave up all to do Thy will,
So may we as loyal children,
   Loyal be and faithful still.

CONCLUDING SERVICE
(Union Prayer Book, page 272)

Recessional

[*Congregation and Confirmands singing as concluding Hymn,*]
"En Kelohenu"

Benediction

Organ Postlude

Confirmation Service

III

ORGAN PRELUDE

SHABUOTH SERVICE
(Union Prayer Book, pages 206-220, 238)

PROCESSIONAL (Organ)—Coronation March........*Meyerbeer*

[Escorted by Confirmands of other years and led by Officials of the Congregation, the Confirmands enter the Temple, each bearing a Bible, a Prayer Book, Six White Rosebuds, and an Emblem of Human Service. The Congregation is requested not to rise during the Processional.]

CHOIR:

How blessed are, how blessed are who come in the name of the
    the Lord our God!
Oh, bless'd be ye, oh, bless'd be ye, in the house of the Lord
    our God.

How blessed are, who come in the name of the Lord our God!
Oh, bless'd be ye, in the house of the Lord our God.

OPENING PRAYER

OUR GOD AND GOD OF OUR FATHERS:

With trembling hearts we approach this sacred altar on this day of our Consecration. We would consecrate our hearts to

Thee. Help us Thou to consecrate also our lives unto Thy service.

We thank Thee for Thy great kindness unto us in permitting us to reach this day. We thank Thee for the understanding which leads us to appreciate its blessing and its sacredness. Bless all who have guided us in the path that leads to this altar. Be with all of them, present and absent, who have loved us and guided us and trained us. For the good they have done us, we are grateful and we beseech Thy blessing for them. And as for us, help us so to live as to make a worthy recompense for all they have done for us.

May the emotions of this hour leave their deep impress on our souls and our minds. May the significance of this hour be deeply graven on the tablets of our hearts. May the reverence of this occasion ever help us to lead noble lives, pious lives, useful lives, and may it so strengthen us as to be able always to resist all temptations and to conquer all evil.

Be Thou with the words of our mouths on this day. May the words which we speak be not merely utterances of lips but honest and true confessions of our hearts. We ask it reverently, we pray fervently. Give us the assurance that Thou art with us and that Thou wilt guide us and love us. Amen.

[*Confirmands deposit within Shrine: Bible, Prayer Book, Emblem of Human Service and Six White Rosebuds.*]

HYMN

[*The Congregation is requested to rise and join in the singing of this and subsequent hymns.*]

Hark, the voice of children
Sounding forth with might,
Judah's sons and daughters
Vow to do the right.

Israel's lofty banner
Leads them to success,
God Himself protects them,
He their vows will bless.

REFRAIN:

Onward, children, onward,
Fearless, firm and true,
Keep your hearts uplifted,
Peace and truth pursue.

Pray'rs and songs of gladness,
In this sacred shrine,
Seal your confirmation,
Crown your faith divine!
Never cease to love it,
And forsake it not;
Wear its shield of honor
Without stain or blot.

REFRAIN:

Onward, children, onward, etc.

Judah, we thy children
Pray for strength and love;
Make us banner bearers,
True to God above.
Gather us together,
'Round thy Torah's light.
Bless thy sons and daughters
Who thy laws recite.

REFRAIN:

Onward, children, onward, etc.

THE TORAH SERVICE
(Union Prayer Book, page 248)

FIRST BENEDICTION
SCRIPTURE: TEN COMMANDMENTS (in Hebrew)
SECOND BENEDICTION
TRANSLATION OF TEN COMMANDMENTS
THE HAPHTARAH (Isaiah 42:1-12)

RETURNING OF THE SCROLL TO THE SHRINE
(Union Prayer Book, page 270)

———

*The addresses of the Confirmands and the Rabbi's charge are
a unit, dealing with the general theme of*

THE JOURNEY OF LIFE

I

GUIDANCE FOR THE JOURNEY

THE ROAD MAP—JEWISH LITERATURE

A familiar scene in a family with an infant is enacted on the
day when the child makes the first effort to walk. The family
is gathered in the living room, watching the baby's antics as
he crawls about on a blanket laid in the middle of the floor.
Suddenly, he catches sight of a glittering object held out to
him. He stretches out a hand for it, but no one pays any
attention. With an eye still on the coveted prize, he rises and
picks his way slowly toward his father's chair. He falls
twice, but both times helping hands set him aright. Once he
bumps into a table and hurts his head, but mother kisses it.

At last, amidst great applause from those assembled, he reaches his goal. The object is his to have and to hold.

From these first steps of the infant, through boyhood and manhood, more steps are taken along the highway of life. But unlike his childish "first steps" a helping hand does not always conduct him, a mother's tender lips do not always comfort him, and a loving audience does not always applaud him. The road of life, a long, winding path with many turnings and some detours, often a lonely road, marked off by mile stones representing years, a road with a mysterious destination—is not an easy one to traverse, and each of us has to explore it for himself. Yet, if one is wise, one may be guided at times by the experience of others, by the experience of those who have gone before. And if such guidance is sought, we discover that we need not go unaided.

Here we are, young Jews, just setting out upon our life's journey. As we start, we are aware that we have had handed down to us a treasury of wisdom, the thoughts, the experiences, the observations, the philosophy, the ideas of generations that have gone before us. These are ours to use, as a road map is used. The route is indicated, the good road, the bad stretches, the detours to be taken or avoided, the dangerous locations, and above all the goal for which we should aim. All of these are indicated on our road map—the Literature of the Jew.

Our Bible, inspired and inspiring, the record of our fathers' quest of the highest good; the Talmud, containing the practical wisdom and legislation of the Rabbis; the literature produced in the great schools of the early centuries, the writings of sages and teachers of all ages, down to our own days; writings which have inspired our fathers through the generations and guided them on to the road of life,—these constitute our cherished road map, for us to read and to heed. These tomes of Jewish Literature form the truest, and most carefully planned map of "The Journey of Life" available to us.

Today we stand at God's altar prepared by those who love us to journey on the Road of Life. We are grateful for the great spiritual treasures which are ours, and for the guidance which will be our joy and inspiration; we are grateful for the influences and incentives which will help us to pursue honorably, daringly and yet hopefully and reverently that Path which now is opened to us.

THE SERVICE STATION—THE SYNAGOGUE

As we start out on this journey of life, even though the road map is before us, some questions arise: Can we expect to go through life without being helped and guided on our journey? Can we expect to go through to the end, without repeated refueling? May we assume that at no time will there be need for adjustments, perhaps repairs? Can we take along sufficient refreshment for the journey without ever needing to replenish? In other words, could we venture upon this journey of life as Jews and feel secure without the assurance also being given to us that service stations are to be found on this journey, that will satisfy the needs and provide the service on the way?

We believe that the Synagogue as it developed through history represents such a service station on the highway of life. We believe that each Synagogue is such a station.

The Synagogue has a threefold aspect. It is the *Beth Hatefilah,* the House of Worship, satisfying our spiritual needs with inspiration and assurance, telling us of God and His will in the universe, telling us of purpose and a goal, giving us hope and confidence to continue our task.

The Synagogue serves as the *Beth Hamidrash,* the House of Learning, where the experiences of the past and of the present are interpreted, and where the road traversed is studied and the right road that is ahead is pointed out to us.

The Synagogue is also the *Beth Hakeneseth,* the Community Center, the rallying point of the Jewish community, the symbol of Jewish unity, the hub about which Jewish life revolves.

It is in the Synagogue—the Service Station on the highway of Jewish Life—that the experts may be found, they who may be expected to tell us what is wrong with our vehicle and might suggest ways of keeping it intact and in functioning condition. They are the custodians of the road maps which have been preserved through history by the Synagogue. They are the interpreters of Torah, the spiritual heritage of the house of Israel. They suggest the adjustments and repairs which make the continuity of Jewish life possible.

The Synagogue—Service Station of the Jew—is always to be found on the highway as we journey through life and it is found wherever Jews are. It welcomes all who would avail themselves of its service. It offers rest to the weary, consolation to the stricken, cheer to the depressed, and hope and guidance to all. However steep the hill we may have to climb; however stony the road; however broken down we may be, or discouraged or disillusioned; on the highway, we shall find one of these Service Stations and there we may find the reassurance that comes through faith and understanding, that perilous though the journey be, the goal is worth the effort and the hardships.

II

THE EQUIPAGE

THE HOME

We have the road maps for the journey. We are assured of Service Stations on the highway. But what shall be the vehicle in which we shall make the journey? What is it that will carry us?

We start our journey in the home and in a real sense we never leave the home. It carries us all through our life. For the influences we find in the home, the love there demonstrated, the ideals which are held before us, the unity and the sanctity of which the Jewish home is so proud, the comradeship which one finds there, the selflessness of service and the wholesomeness of influence, these carry us through until the end.

The Jewish home has been a refuge and a haven for the Jew through all the ages. Whatever the outside world offered to him, within the home he found dignity and was recognized and dealt with as a human being. In the midst of the prosaic life about him, his home introduced to him the poetry of being. Into the sordidness of life, the home introduced the beauty and charm of sacred life. Into all matters secular, the Jewish home radiated the value and reality of holiness. To all living and experience, it gave meaning and consecration. These influences one does not discard, one cannot. They carry us even as we preserve them.

Such has been the Jewish home of the past. From such homes we come. These are the homes that send us out into life. These are the homes that will carry us. May we be worthy of this advantage.

Society

Though we are born into a home and by its influence are carried on through life, the home itself is part of a larger group, namely, the human family or Society. As soon as we pass the first few years of helplessness we begin to have contacts with this larger group in the neighborhood, in the school, in the larger and greater contacts in business, in industry, in commerce, in the professions, in world affairs. And it is in society, using the word in this broadest sense of the fellowship of all men, that we truly travel through life. This, too, is a vehicle of life.

And if we are to travel in it, it becomes, very clearly, our responsibility to see to it that this vehicle, Society, functions properly and in all of its parts. It must be fuelled and heated; it must be kept sanitary and clean; impurities must be eliminated and wholesome and decent standards of existence should prevail for all those who with us are using this vehicle.

We, ourselves, are in duty bound so to live and conduct ourselves that we may not become burdens unto others, and we should also strive to make circumstances for our fellow human beings such that they may not be compelled to clog life mentally, morally and physically. To do this, we must hold ourselves responsible not alone for our own lives, but for the happiness and peace, for the joys and opportunities, for the security and comfort of all others traveling with us. We must "know how the other half lives," and knowing it we must help them make their life meaningful and wholesome.

This it is to keep the vehicle in good condition, and we should do it, as the Rabbis always taught us, by serving God and man without the expectation of reward, our compensation being the good life, the useful life itself.

Our journey through life will be pleasanter for all just as our ride in any vehicle like an automobile is more pleasant when the machinery is oiled and greased and in good working condition.

RELIGION

The journey through life can be made most attractive when we take it in the vehicle of the highest and noblest ideals. As we understand Religion and particularly our own Religion, Judaism, it represents the highest idealism man can conceive, for Religion is a reaching out after communion with God who is perfection, the supreme of goodness and beauty and love and happiness.

The noblest ideals for man are taught by Religion. To do justice, to love mercy, to walk humbly, to love our neighbors, and the strangers, to protect the helpless, to shelter the homeless, to pursue peace and to bear no grudges, to be holy usefully, that is Religion translated into deeds. And to travel through life with this idealism, with these values applied and realized in life is to travel in a vehicle that is high-powered and to go on a journey that is exhilarating.

Some people think of Religion as merely a matter of "faith without works." Judaism was never that. It always has stressed the idea that our works and deeds must ever be motivated by our faith. Some think and say that Judaism is a religion of the past dealing only with what is gone and not with what is to be. That is not so, for using our Judaism as a vehicle through life we are going from the past, through the present, toward greater achievements in the future. The best is not in the past, the noblest is yet to be.

On this journey, difficulties will be encountered, unfavorable weather, poor roads, difficulties with the vehicle, and so on. There will be moments of disheartenment, perhaps moments of discouragement. It will be in those moments that refuge will be needed, inner protection will be required to help the traveler.

It is Religion that then will help us most. It is through it that peace of soul may be acquired and courage and hope attained for the future. It will be in those darker hours that Religion will "cause light to shine over the earth and all its inhabitants," ourselves included.

Hymn

God of Israel, keep us faithful to Thy holy laws;
We would join with earnest brothers in Thy cause.

We would strive to be a blessing to the human race,
Thee before all men professing, God of grace.

Let no worldly pomp or pleasure lead our hearts astray,
Kinder make us, Lord, more faithful day by day.

Soldiers of the light upholding Israel's sacred cause,
We would battle, God and Father, for Thy Laws.

III

THE PASSENGERS

Our People Through History

As we set out upon the journey of life, it is not as though we are the first passengers to enter the equipage. Life does not begin here and now. It is only that the vehicle pauses here that new passengers may join those already in it.

Who are they whom we will find aboard?

Viewed from our Jewish angle, we see not alone mankind there, all men, all races, all religions, who have been journeying these many, many years. We see also our people who for 4,000 years have been upon the highway of life, beginning in remote antiquity, and who, by the grace of God, will continue into the unknown future.

During their journey, the experiences of our people have been varied. They have known the heat of the tropics and the freezing blasts of the North. They have had companions who dealt with them kindly and as with human beings, and others who were brutal and arrogant and distressing.

They have journeyed through sunlit territory and have gone through the dense darkness and dampness of caves. They have lived intensely, dreamed nobly, and hoped even when there seemed no warrant for hopefulness.

In amazing profusion, they produced men and women who from Abraham, the idol breaker, through Moses, the law-giver, through David, the nation builder, through Isaiah and Jeremiah, the seers and visionaries, through the Maccabeans, battlers for freedom of conscience, through the Rabbis, the saviours of our people, through sages, philosophers, poets, leaders have given light and hope to their own people and through them to the world.

With a sublime faith in their destiny, believing themselves to be the first-born in the spiritual family of life, the witnesses to a living God, the priests dedicated to service, our people have journeyed through history and come down through the centuries, even unto this moment when a new generation is joining the pilgrimage which extends from antiquity into eternity.

We, Today

And so today, we, of the new generation, are joining those who have traveled through these millennia.

> "Every golden deed of theirs
> Sheds its luster on my way;
> All their labors, all their prayers,
> Sanctify this present day.

> "Heir of all that they have earned
> By their passion and their tears;
> Heir of all that they have learned
> Through the weary, toiling years.

"Heir of all the faith sublime
On whose wings they soared to heaven;
Heir of every hope that time
To earth's fainting sons hath given."

We join the pilgrimage. Will we be worthy of them? They welcome us eagerly, they receive us with hope, with prayers, with joy and with tears.

We, today, will we be worthy of all that the past has wrought? Are we deserving of the confidence reposed in us? Will we be additions of strength or a weakening burden? Will we strengthen the link of all the generations or will we break the continuity?

These are questions our people on their journey through life are asking even now concerning us, the newest passengers entering their midst.

We are proud of the privilege to join the noble company receiving us. And we ask them and you, our dear ones and friends, to be lovingly patient, to strengthen us by your example, to challenge us by your expectations, to strengthen us by your demands of us, and to continue your training that we may fully and honorably take our place in your midst, and that we may bear with you the yoke of the Kingdom of Heaven long ago placed upon our people.

IV

BEGINNING THE JOURNEY

DECLARATION OF FAITH AND VOW

As we start upon our journey now, what are our plans, our ideals, our intentions? We have had ten years of training and preparation for this event. During the last of these years, we had, in addition, the guidance and instruction of our Rabbi. We were confirmed in our faith and in our loyalty even before we came here today. Now we wish but to tell you of that which is in our hearts and publicly to confess our faith, to proclaim our allegiance, and to make our vows.

We accept the obligations of Jewishness and the teachings of Judaism. We mean to live by those ideals and to fulfill our responsibilities. We know the task is not easy. Our Rabbi told us, and from our own observation we know that the Philistines are still challenging us and their Goliaths are still taunting the hosts of the Lord. It behooves us to be unafraid. It is our task to accept the challenge and, like David of old, we shall attempt to go forth to meet our Goliaths and, God helping us, to acquit ourselves in such a manner as to bring honor to our people, blessings to mankind, and glory to our God.

We shall try to be loyal to our companions on this journey. We shall seek to keep the vehicles of life functioning nobly. We mean to use the road maps offered to us and the service stations awaiting us. To our people, we would be loyal. Of our people's ideals, we would be the worthy custodians. Humbly and reverently, we would walk before God, doing justice, loving mercy, living at peace with our neighbors, helping all who need our help, serving wherever the call to service be sounded.

These are our intentions as we begin the journey. This the faith that stirs us and the hopes that lure us. Sincerely, we consecrate ourselves to the best and noblest in life. With full knowledge of what is involved, with understanding of what was imparted to us, and of our own will, we pledge you our loyalty. And rising now in this House of God, on this altar dedicated to His name, before the Torah, symbol of His truth, before you, our nearest and dearest, in the light of history and before the world, we proclaim our faith and make our vow:

[*The Confirmands rise and recite in unison.*]

"I consecrate my life to my people and to my people's faith. With all my heart, with all my soul, and with all my might will I endeavor to further the lofty aims of Judaism and to practice the ideals of the Jew.

"Unto the end of my days, Israel's watchword shall be the slogan of my life and that which it represents will be my guide and inspiration: *Shema Yisroel, Adonoi Elohenu, Adonoi Echod*—Hear, O Israel, the Lord our God, the Lord is One."

CHOIR:

"*Boruch Shem K'vod Malchuso L'olom Vo'ed*"

(Praised be His name whose glorious Kingdom is forever and ever)

V

THE BAGGAGE

WHAT SHALL WE TAKE WITH US?
(*Confirmation Charge by the Rabbi*)

MY DEAR PUPILS:

In but a little while, I shall send you forth stirred and consecrated upon your journey. You know the route which you should follow. You are familiar with the vehicles in which you are going. You know with whom you are to go and what is expected of you on your journey. You have made your declaration and given your vow of faithfulness.

It is now my joyous privilege to give you a word of counsel ere you set forth and I choose to speak of the baggage, of that which you take with you.

I

You take with you your physical heredity. This is a very important factor. Unlike Venus, you have not sprung from the foam of the tempestuous sea. You are not a new creation. You are progeny, you are offspring. You are the latest generation of an ancient people, a people that has been on the march through history for upwards of 4,000 years. You are bone of their bone and tissue of their tissue. In you, physically, their generations converge. I want you to realize that the glow of light that is found in your eyes is borrowed from their past. I look into your eyes and I see in them the flame, the sparkle, the smouldering of generations of Jewish suffering and hoping. I see your eyes melt and move and soften with generations of Jewish tears and thought and aspirations. I see in you, boys, Jewish manhood, enterprising, loyal, undefeated—through the centuries. I see in you, girls, Jewish womanhood, the loveliness of Jewish mothers, the soulfulness of priestesses, officiating at the home altars. These are all part of your physical make-up. They are part of that heredity which you may abuse or pollute but which you cannot disown. This is all part of you. It is not a burden to the loyal, it is not a yoke to them who are worthy; it is rather a precious privilege.

This, your physical heredity, you take with you as you start upon your journey.

II

And you take with you also your spiritual heritage.

The Jew is not alone a physical being. The Jew is unique in that he is not body alone nor soul alone, but is a combination of both. The Jew who is that, only physically, is a pathetic creature. The complete Jew is the physical container of a spiritual glory.

What is this spiritual heritage to which you have fallen heir? I will tell you.

When the rest of the world was still steeped in the crassest superstitions and the most degrading idolatry, it was a son of our people, Elijah, the Prophet, who heard the voice of God speak to him in the soft and quiet whisper of his soul.

When injustice was rampant and corruption filled the land, it was Amos, the Prophet, who hurled his challenge at the heads of King and priest and populace, to dare to do justice.

When coldness and heartlessness were the rule in human relations, the Prophet, Hosea, sounded the message of divine love and divine tenderness.

When war was deemed the honored and essential occupation of men and nations, the Prophets of your people and mine, Isaiah and Micah, visioned and spoke of an age when the nations of the world would learn war no more.

When ignorance and illiteracy abounded among the masses of the peoples, the Rabbis of Israel fostered universal education in Jewish life and built renowned academies.

When selfishness was the rule, Jewish sages taught the highest law of altruism, of selfless service. "Be ye not like servants who serve their master for the sake of reward. Be ye rather like unto those who serve their master without the expectation of reward." And Jewish philanthropy as *Tzedaḳah,* as justice and righteousness, taught the world a priceless lesson in social responsibility and kindliness.

When in the Middle Ages, immorality was almost fostered, within Ghetto walls Jewish homes were sanctuaries where purity and chastity and the beauty of holiness held sway. During those same ages, when illiteracy was the rule, Jewish education kept our people literate and taught them to cherish learning and to honor the scholar above all. *"Torah—Hee Orah"—"Knowledge is Light."* That was the Jewish precept!

Wherever there was suffering, there the Jew commiserated. Wherever there was oppression, there the Jew yearned for freedom. And always and everywhere, he found himself as he believed himself to be *"tachath kanphai hashekinah"—"under the protection of divinity,"* and adored the everlasting God and rendered Him his praise.

In the valley of the shadow the Jew feared no evil, and in joy he thanked Him, by whose will everything was created. Always the Jew communed with his God, in the night watches as well as in every conscious moment.

III

This is the heritage which with your heredity are yours. Be this the baggage you take with you on your journey. And as symbolic of these, I return to you that which you have deposited in the Ark.

In token of your God consciousness, I give you your Prayer Book. Use it!

In token of your Jewish loyalty and your attachment to learning and ideals, I return your Bible to you. Read it, study it, absorb it.

In token of your social responsibility and your service, I return to you your pin with the word "Service" thereon. Wear it not only, but render service.

This is the threefold cord of Jewish values. God, Israel, man. Your task is clear.

Remember this, however, that by reason of your heredity and heritage, you, as Jews, can fulfil yourselves only through Israel. Israel is *your* medium for living. And in token of this, I give back to you now, your six white rosebuds, symbolizing the six letters in the word *Israel*.

Let the first, standing for the letter *I,* speak to you of *Innocence.* I bid you bring this rose with you and deposit it in the

Ark when you come here in a little while to receive your blessing. Let it be your solemn pledge made on this great day to lead lives that are pure and unpolluted.

Let the second bud, representing the letter *S*, tell you of the *Sacrifices* which your parents have made in your behalf. Give this rose to them and let it be your assurance of your appreciation, and of your resolution to be worthy of their sacrifices.

Let the third rose, standing for the letter *R*, speak of *Religion*. Give that rose to me, your Rabbi, in token of your pledge to live the life that is religious and to be faithful to the precepts and challenge of religion.

Let the next flower standing for the letter *A*, suggest the virtue of *Altruism*. Give that one to some philanthropic institution in token of your determination to share life with others and to make it meaningful for others.

Let the next rosebud stand for the letter *E* and the word *Education*. Give that to one of your teachers whose good opinion you respect the most. Ask her or him to preserve that rose as a token of the pledge you give to keep your mind ever open, eager, questing, to continue learning as you live.

And the last rose, standing for the letter *L* and the word *Labor*, I suggest that you keep yourself. Put it where you may see it occasionally and let it be a constant reminder unto you to lead a life which shall be characterized by useful and honorable toil.

This, my dear young friends, is your baggage. This you take with you as you set out upon your journey. Richly endowed you go forth. God grant that when you reach the end on your journey, your life will have been such that the heritage you will transmit to others will be greatly and nobly enriched.

And now, as you go, I give you this for your motto:

"Be not wise in your own hearts,
Fear the Lord and depart from evil." (Prov. 3:7.)

To Truth and its pursuit, to God and the love of Him, to Man and his ennoblement, to Israel and his service, I now dedicate you! "Go forth in this your strength and redeem Israel. Behold, it is I who send you." (Judg. 6:7.)

In the name of God, then, approach the shrine!

[*At the conclusion of the Charge, the Emblems deposited in the Ark are returned. When the children are seated, the Congregation unites in singing.*]

HYMN

Suppliant low, Thy children bend,
Father, for Thy blessing now;
Thou canst teach us, guide, defend;
We are weak, almighty Thou.

With the peace Thy word imparts
Be the taught and teachers blest;
In our lives and in our hearts,
Father, be Thy laws impressed.

Grant us spirits lowly, pure,
Errors pardoned, sins forgiven;
Humble trust, obedience sure,
Love to man, and faith in Heaven.

VI

A BLESSING FOR THE JOURNEY—THE RABBI

VII

THE CLOSING PRAYER

O LORD, OUR GOD:

Once again we thank Thee for the inspiration of this day, for the emotions that have surged through our hearts, for every thought that blessed us and every memory that stirred us.

As we go forth, do Thou guide our footsteps so that we may not stray from the path of duty. Give us the vision to see the light of faith, of ideals, of spiritual values which our Judaism holds out before us, and may we have the courage and the wisdom faithfully to follow that light. Give us the strength of character and the discernment of judgment to choose the path of righteousness and ever to follow it.

When we first entered this Religious School, we had little conception of Thine infinite greatness and wisdom. Year by year as we came here, we grew in knowledge and in under-standing and we learned to appreciate Thy goodness and the marvel of Thy mighty deeds. We learned of the comfort of Thy teachings and of the sustaining power of Thy wisdom. And today, as we go forth upon the journey of life, we pray unto Thee, Father of mercies, lover of Thy children, to be with us, to hold us in Thy love, to guide us in Thy way, to cheer us by Thy providence and to comfort us by the assurance that Thou art ever watchful over us and wilt lead us in safety unto our destination.

We know that the path may not always be easy. We know of some of the trials that we should expect. We have been warned that there will be those who will seek to tempt us from the path of righteousness and goodness. Help us to resist the snare and the temptations on the way. And may ours be the joy of knowing that we dared to do the right, although the wrong may have seemed the easier.

For the blessing and love of our parents, for the affectionate guidance of our Rabbi and teachers, for the example set before us by good men and women everywhere, we thank Thee truly, sincerely.

May the words of our mouth and meditations of our heart on this day and in this hour be acceptable in Thy sight, who art our Rock, our Fortress, our Redeemer.

Amen.

HYMN

Lord, before Thy sacred Altar
 At the Temple's holy shrine,
Come Thy children with devotion
 To beseech Thy grace divine.
Here we pledge our consecration
 To the Law Thou didst reveal.
O may nations all revere it
 As life's holiest ideal.

O confirm our faith's devotion
 To Thy sacred Law of truth;
To the vow our fathers rendered
 In our peoples' early youth.
So we vow, in faith enduring,
 To be steadfast to the trust,
Which at Sinai they accepted,
 Which accept we will and must.

And while men in great contention
 Still withhold to sing Thy praise,
May Thine ancient faithful people,
 Lead the nations in Thy ways.
As our fathers greatly suffering,
 Gave up all to do Thy will,
So may we as loyal children,
 Loyal be and faithful still.

CONCLUDING SERVICE
(Union Prayer Book, page 272)

RECESSIONAL

[*Congregation and Confirmands singing as Concluding Hymn*]
"En Kelohenu"

BENEDICTION

ORGAN POSTLUDE